Fun at

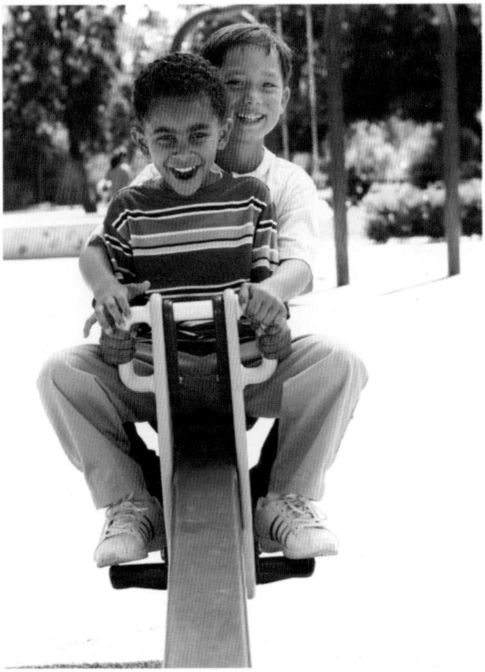

written by Pam Holden

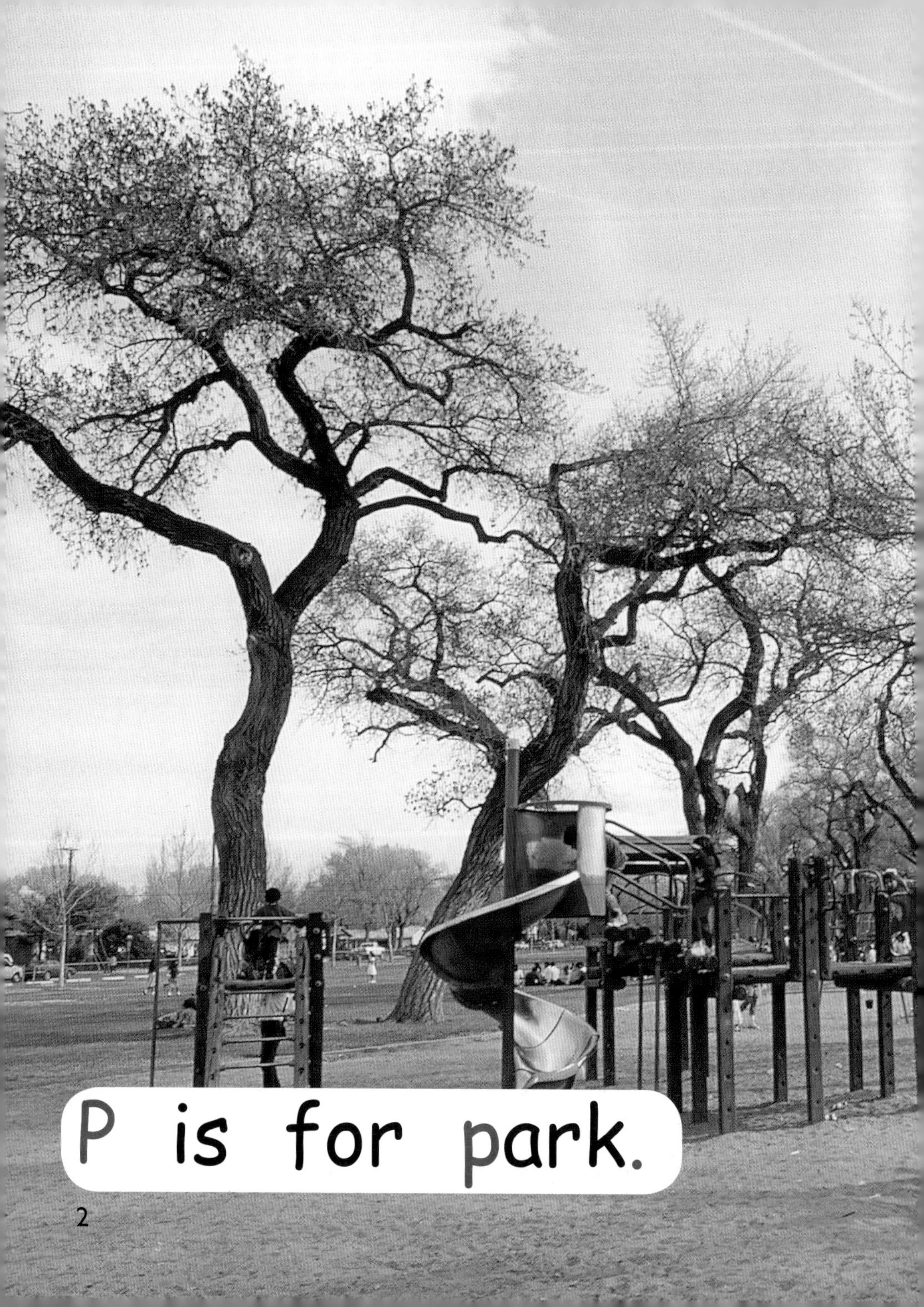

P is for park.

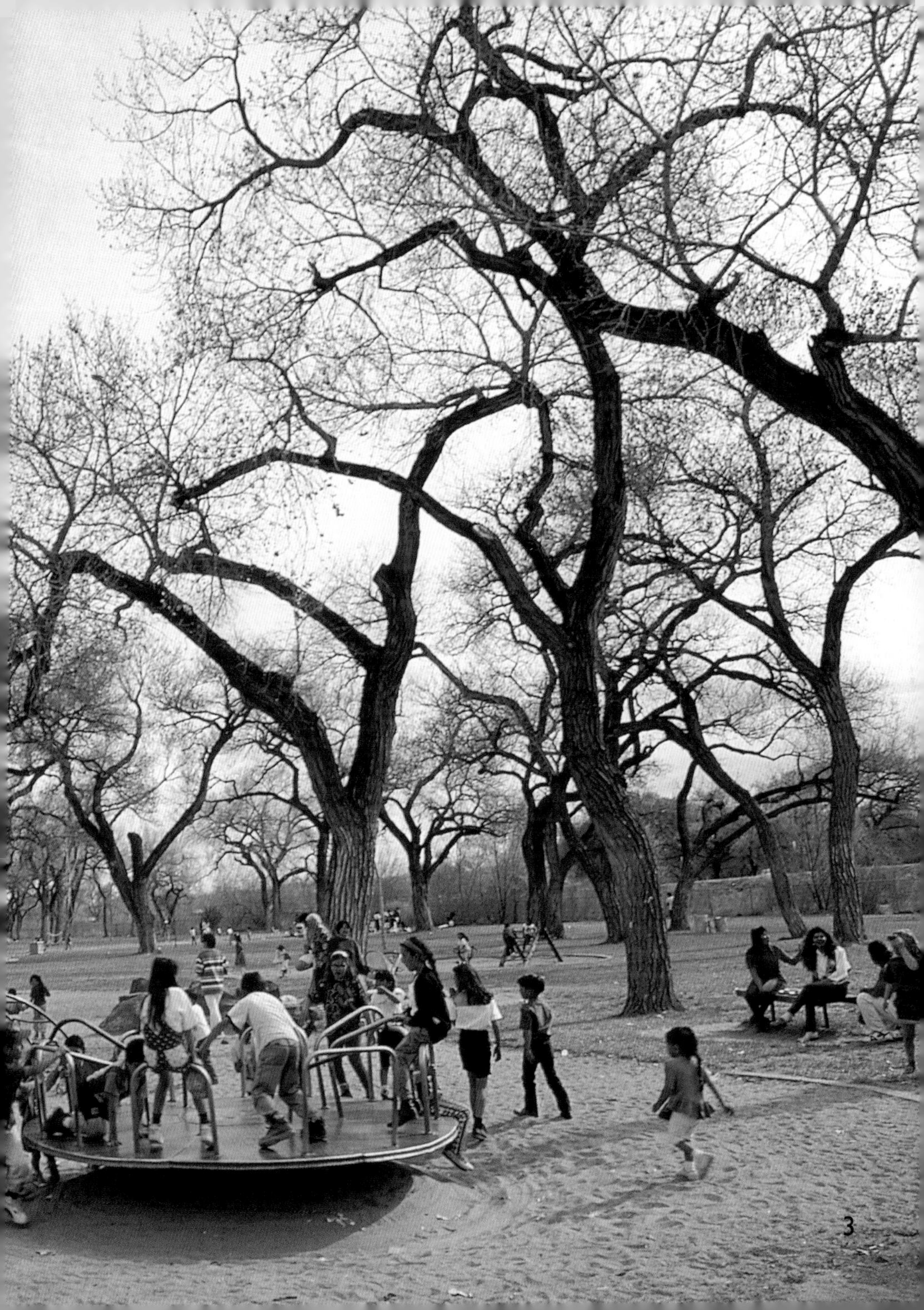

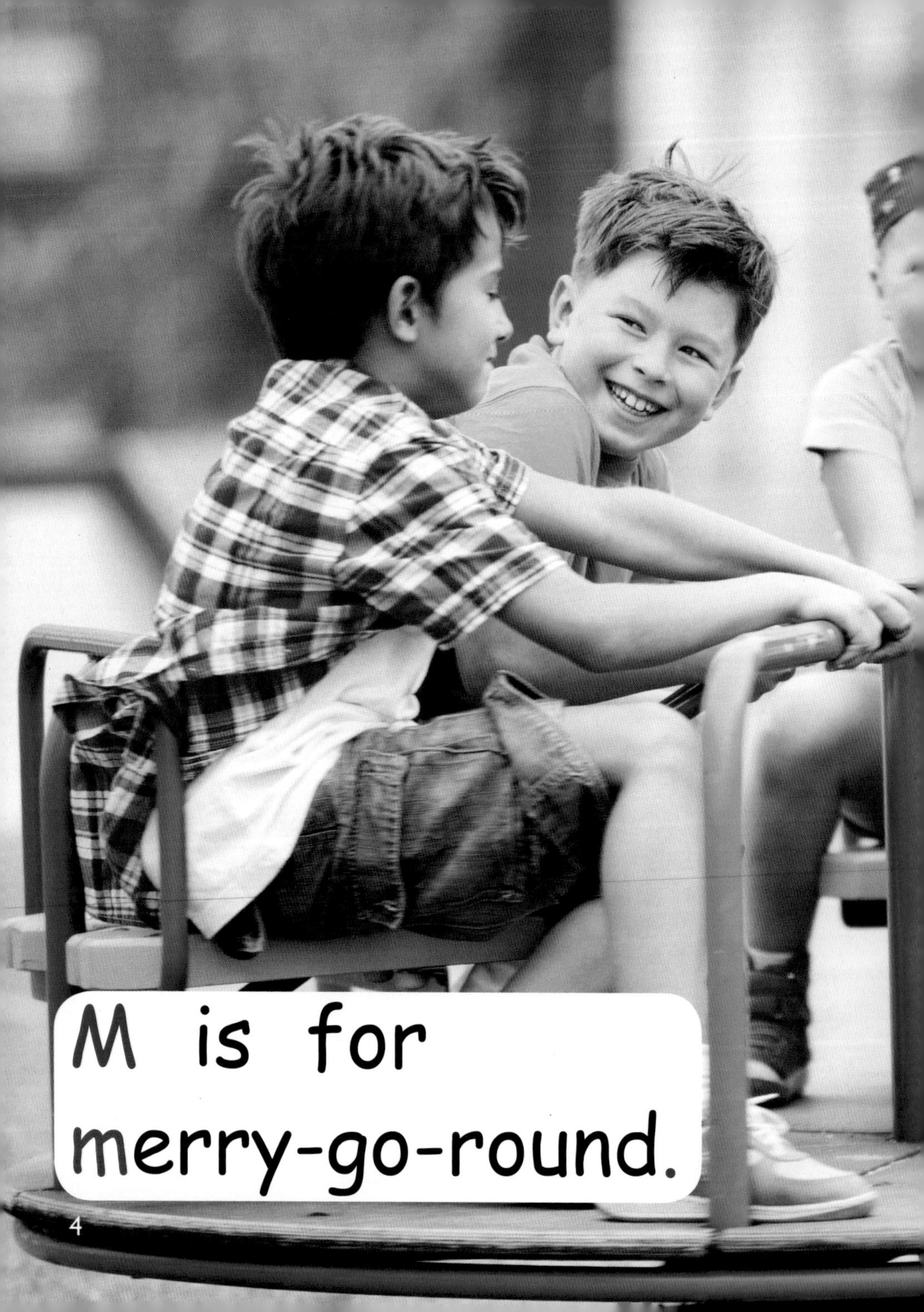

M is for
merry-go-round.

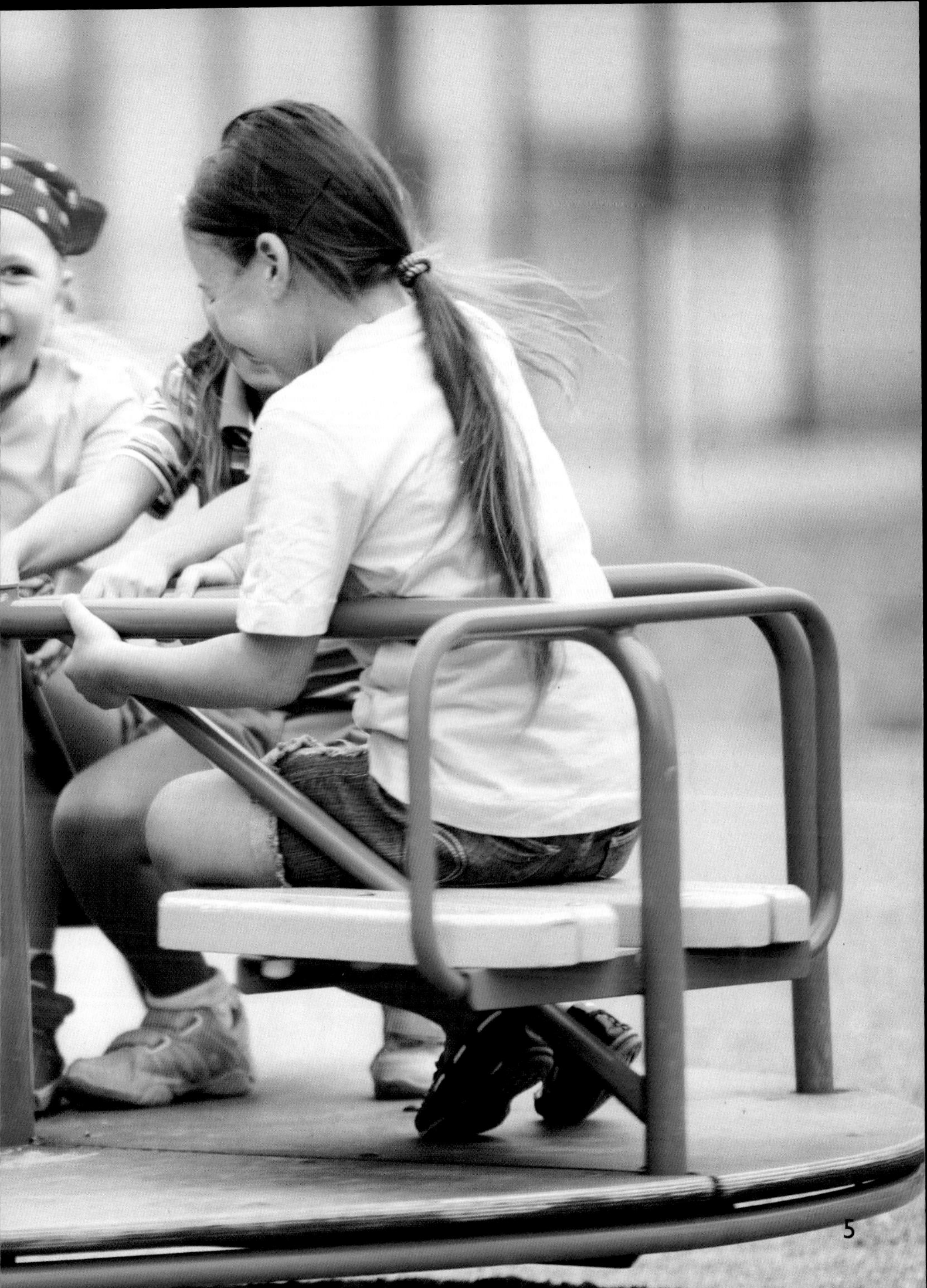

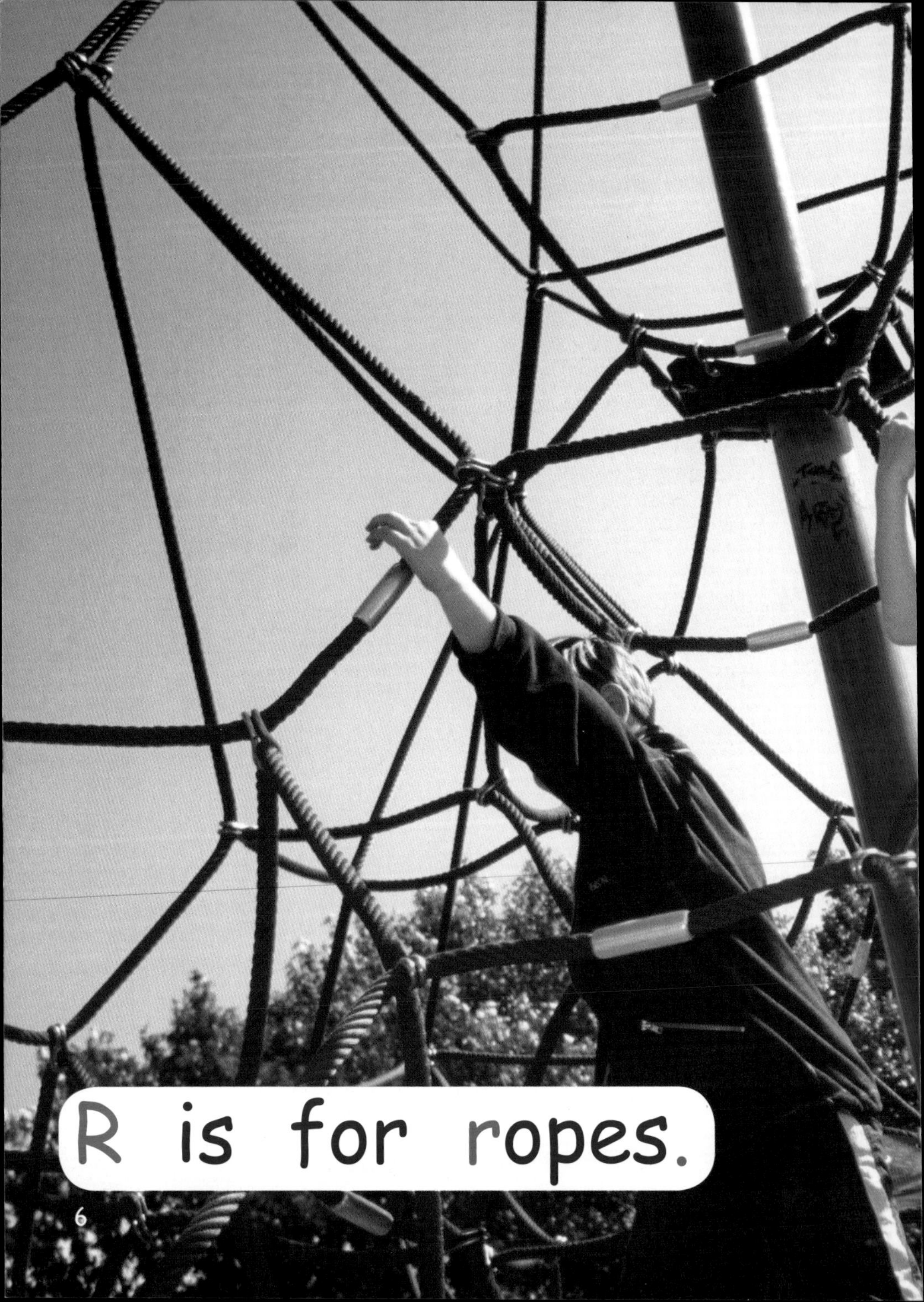

R is for ropes.

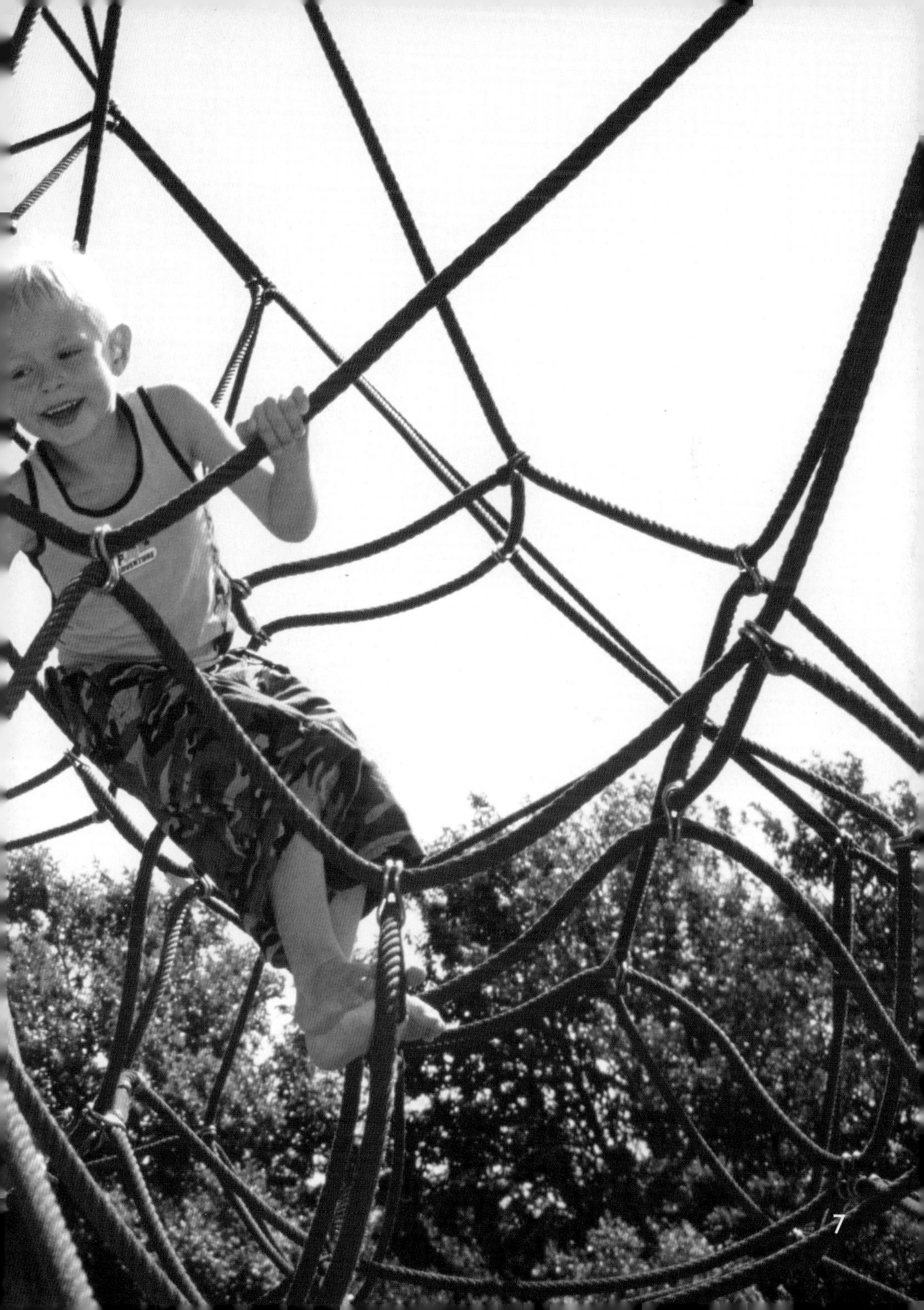

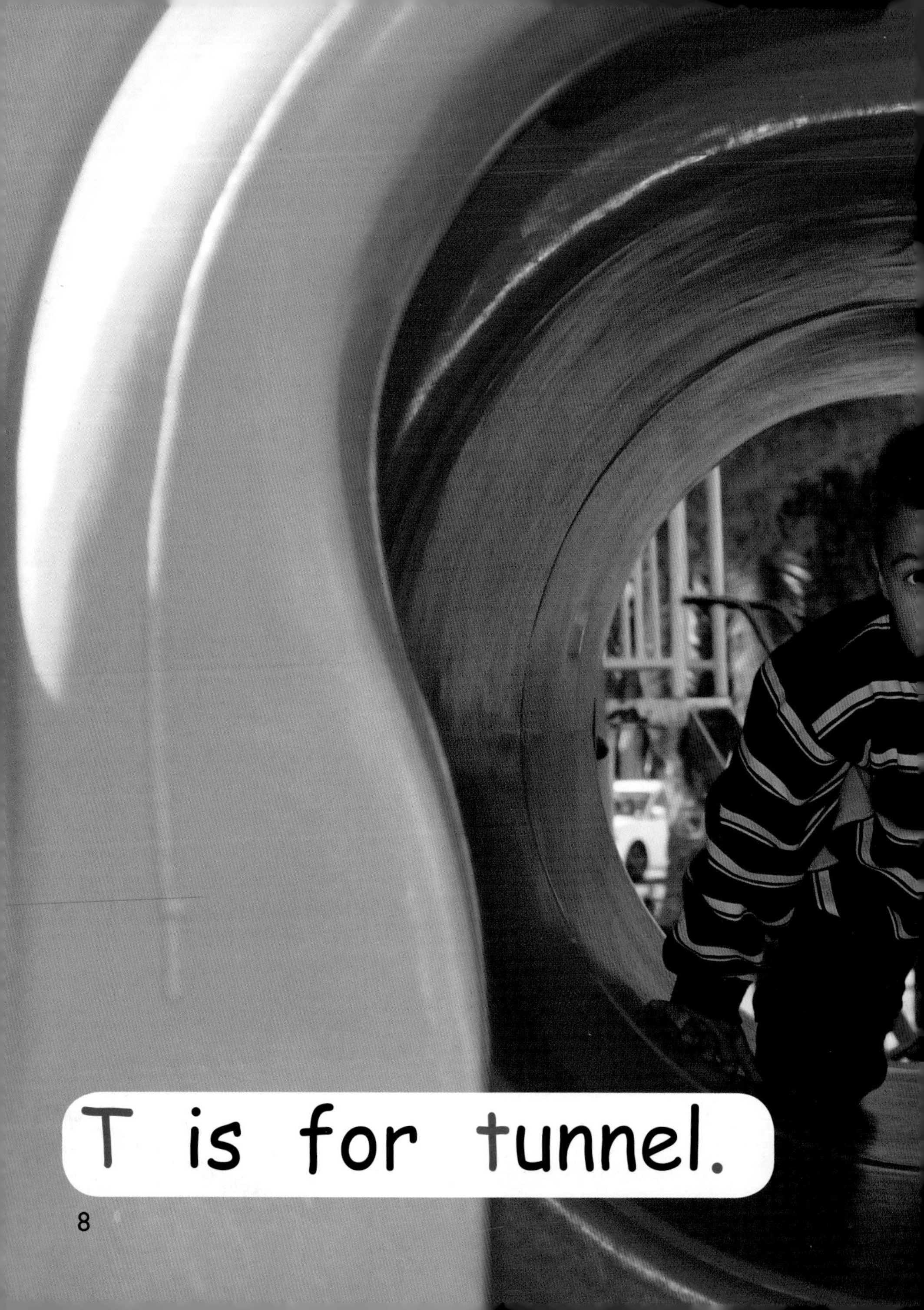

T is for tunnel.

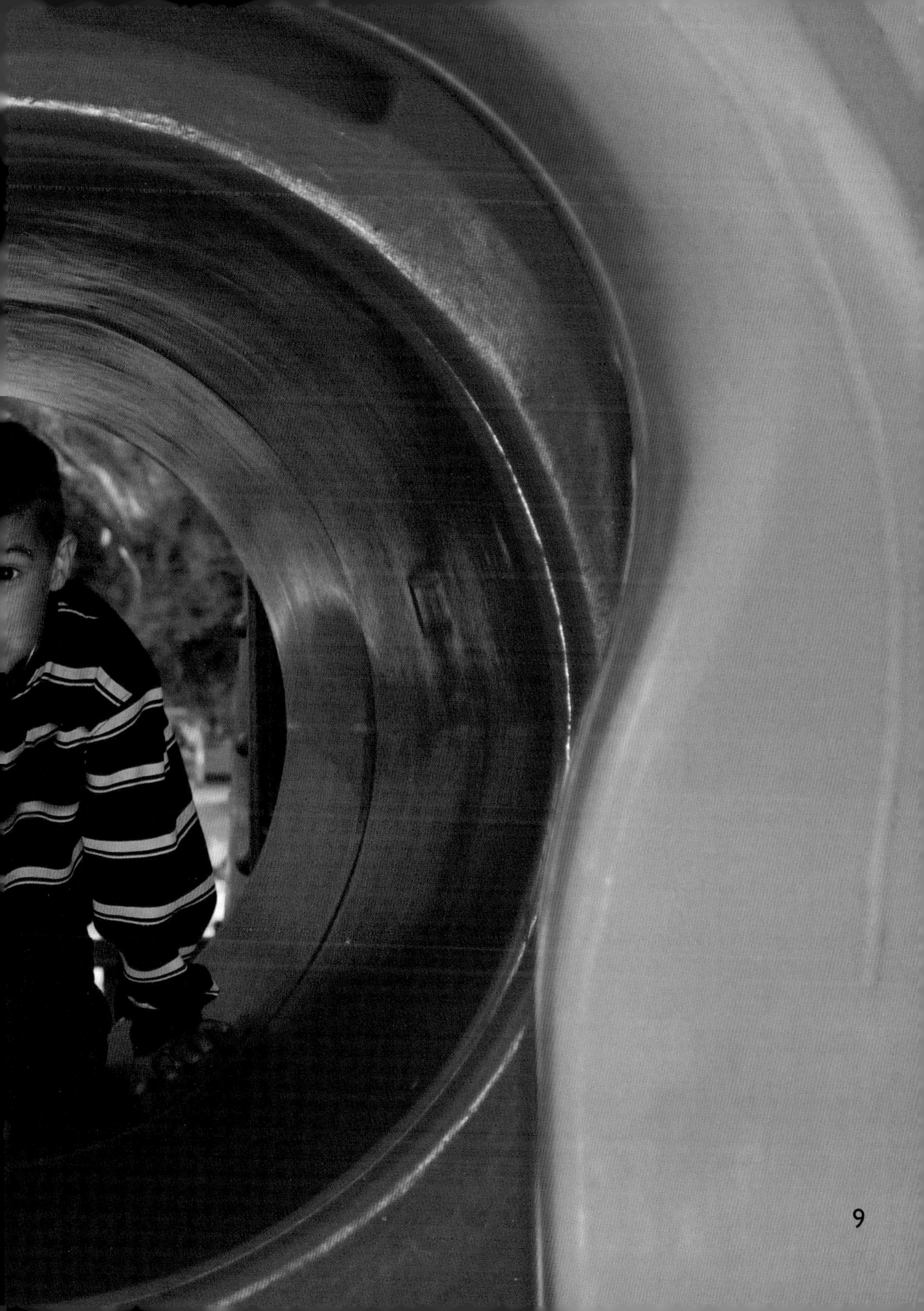

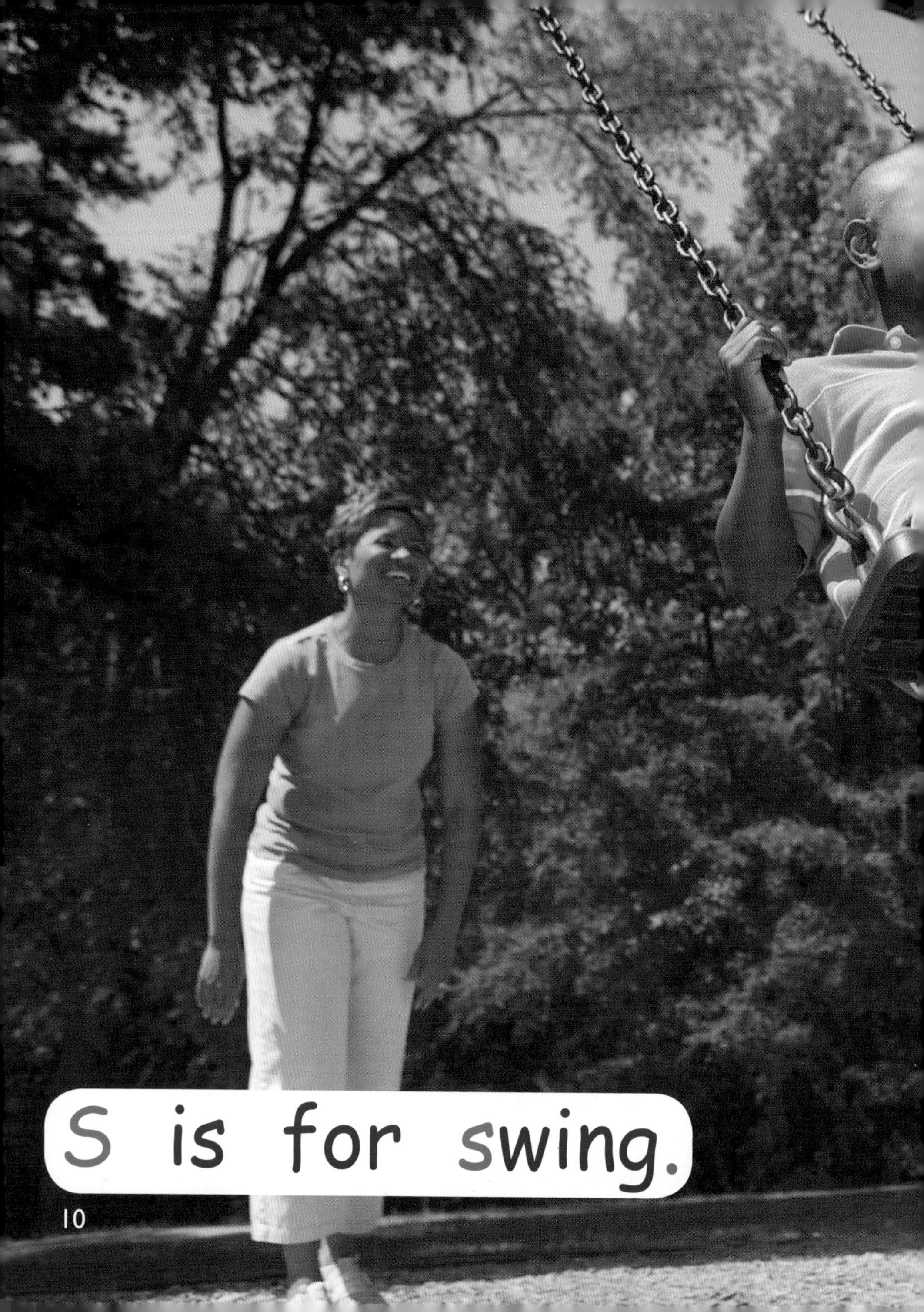

S is for swing.

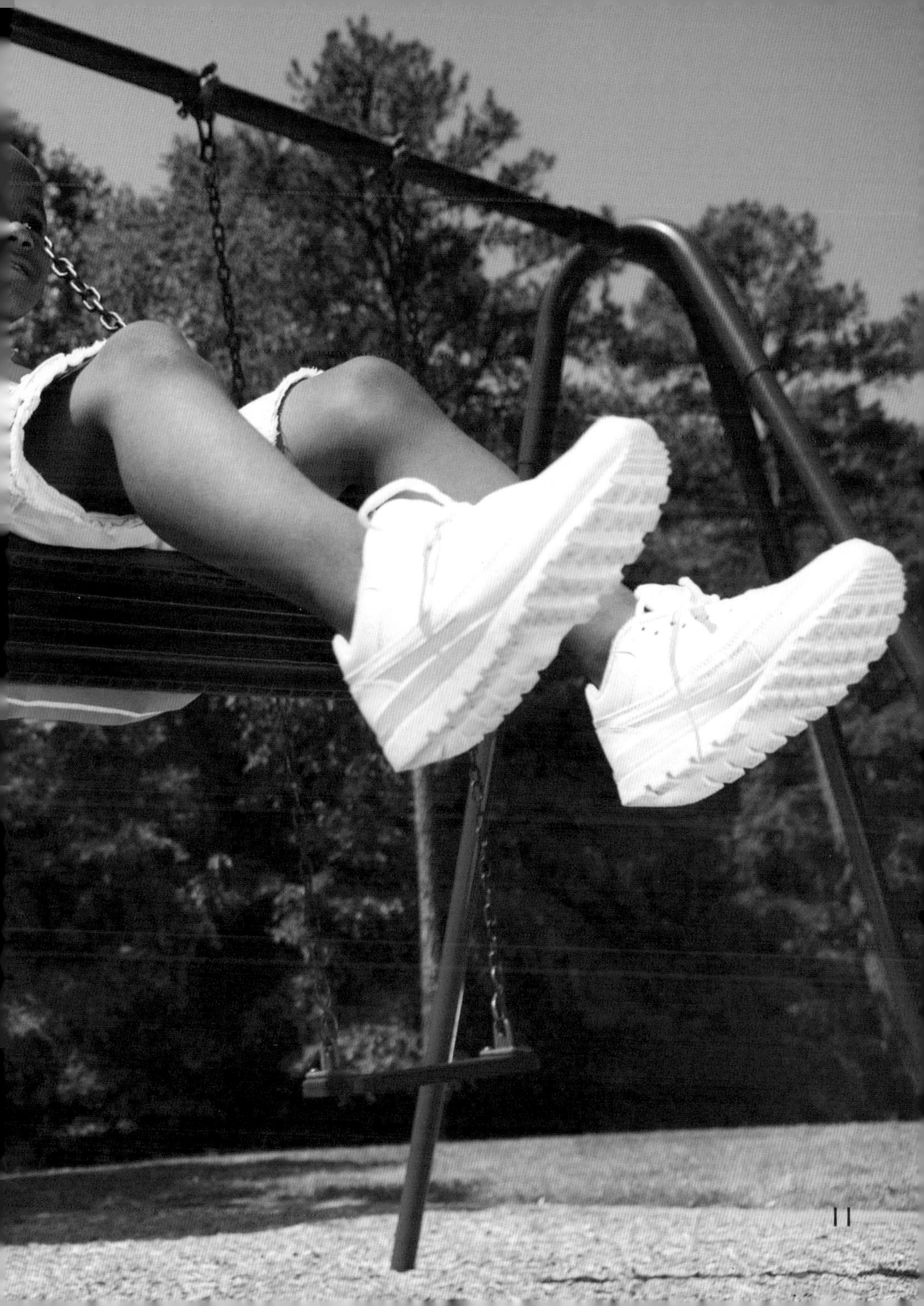

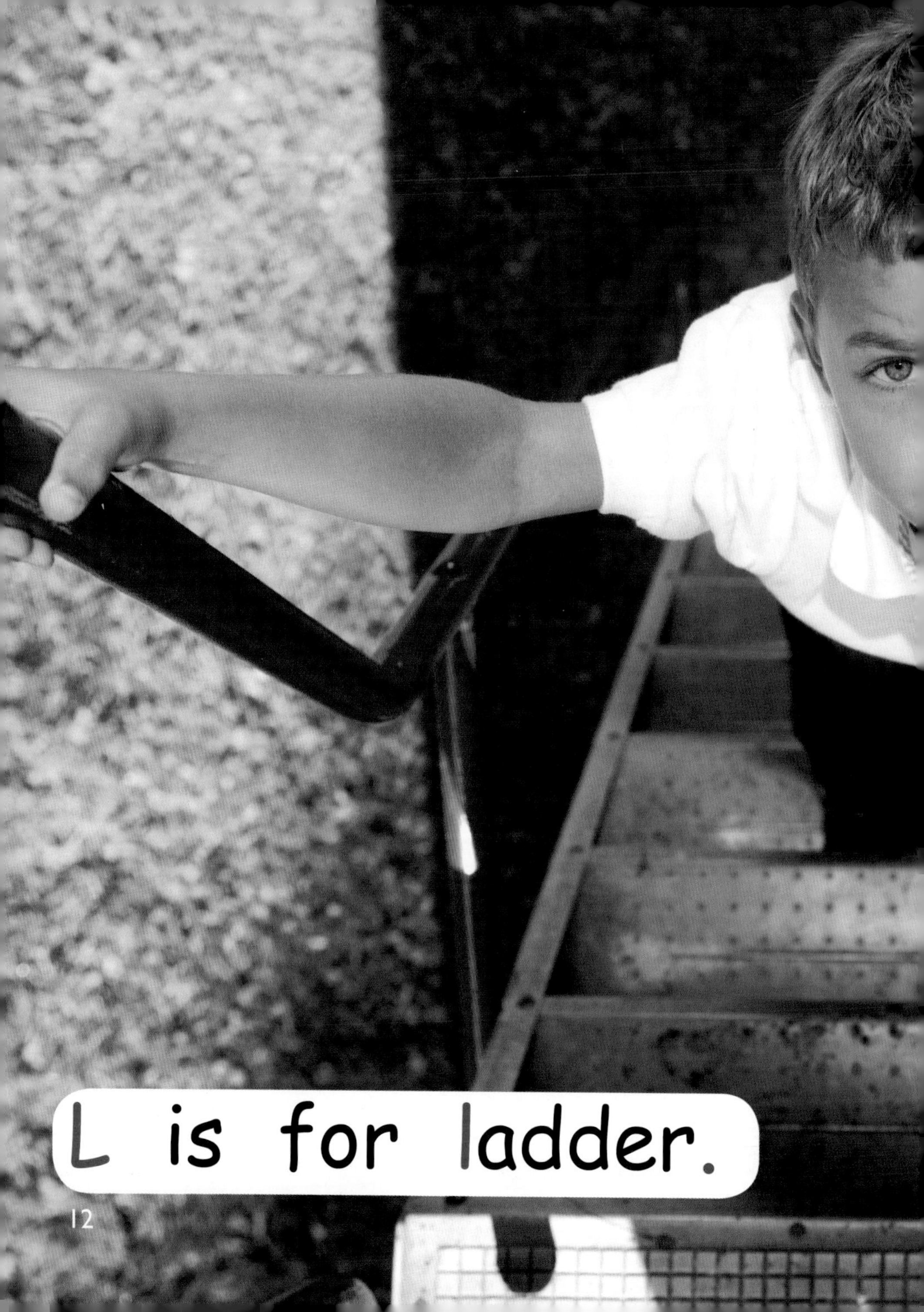

L is for ladder.

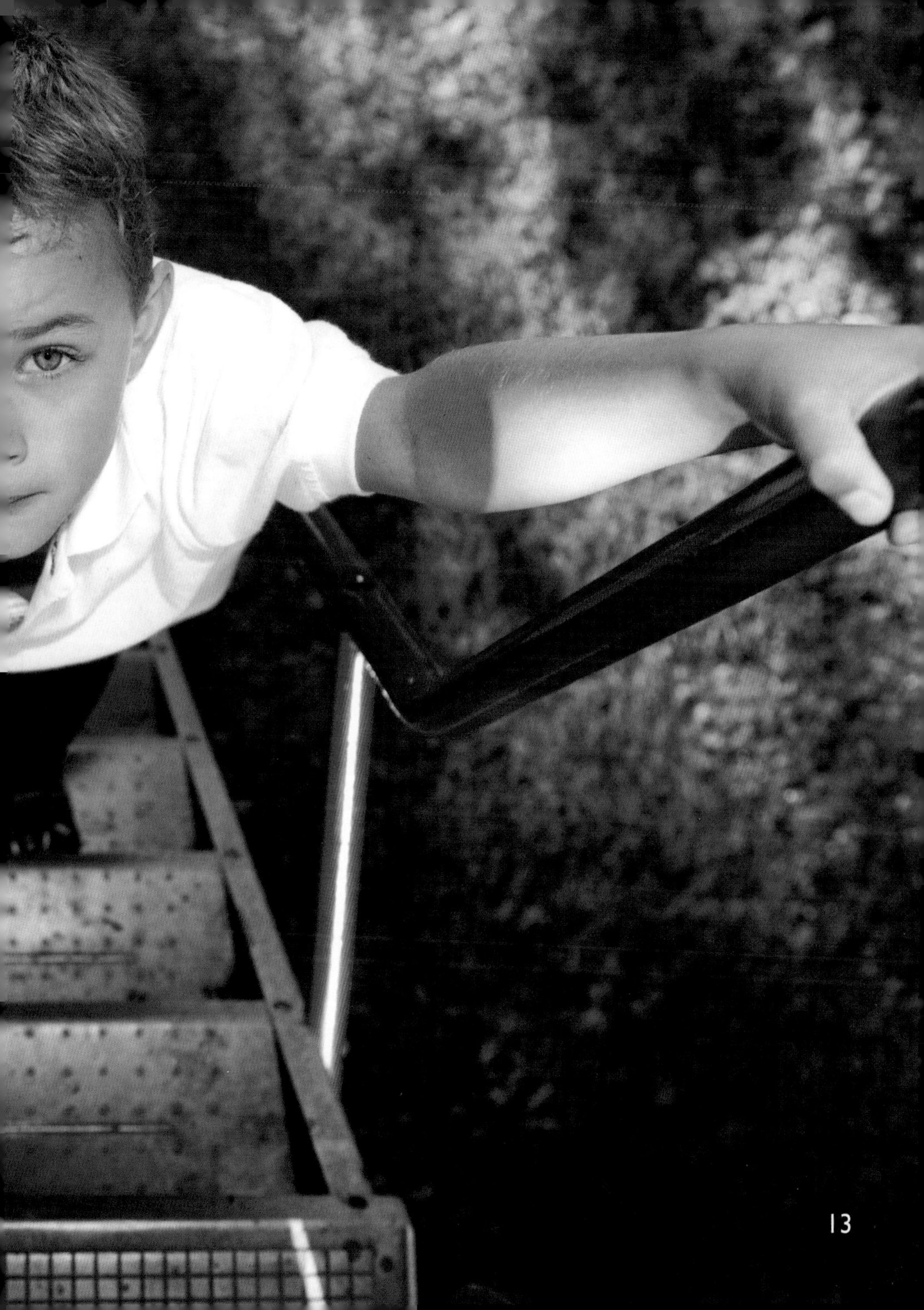

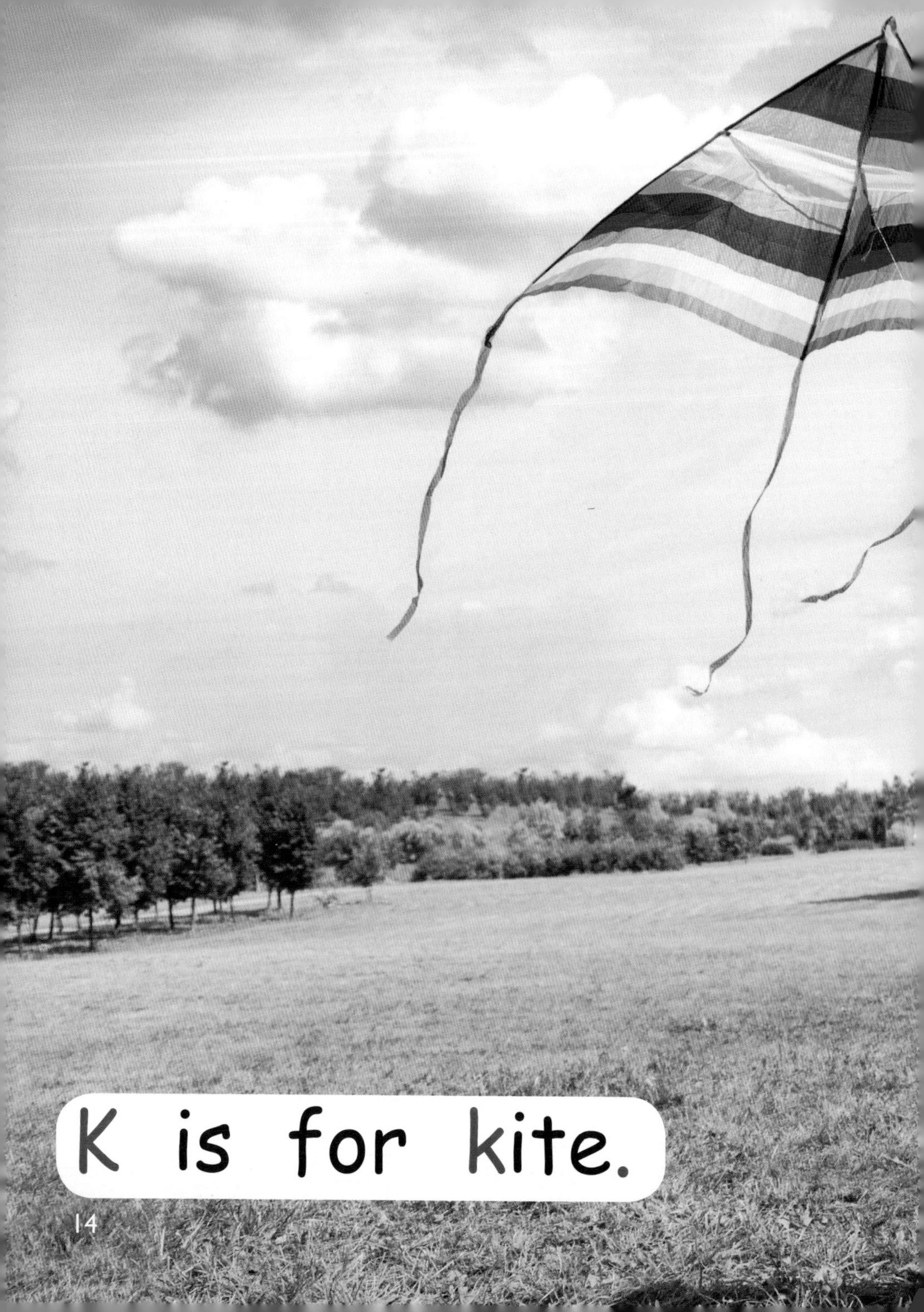

K is for kite.

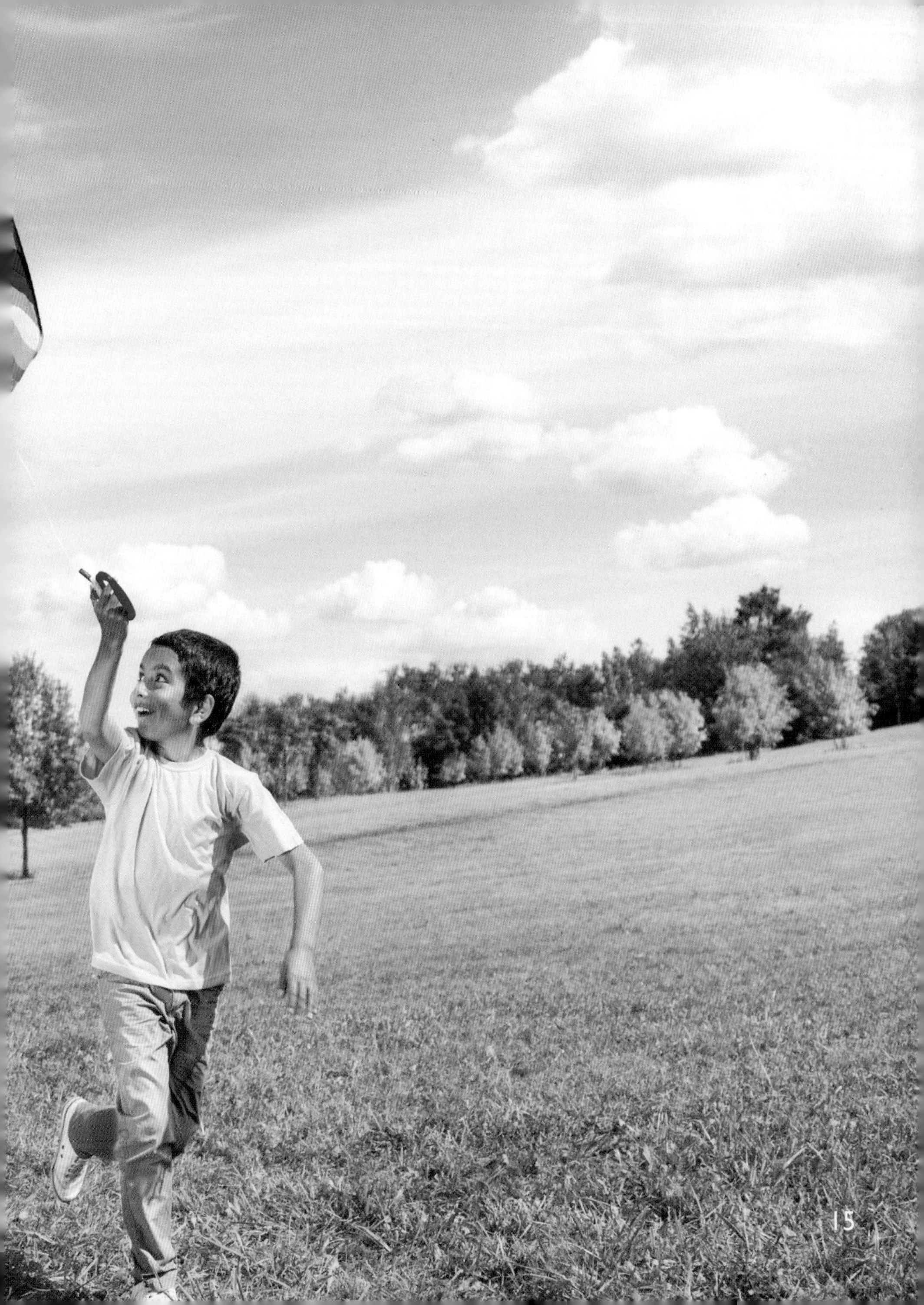

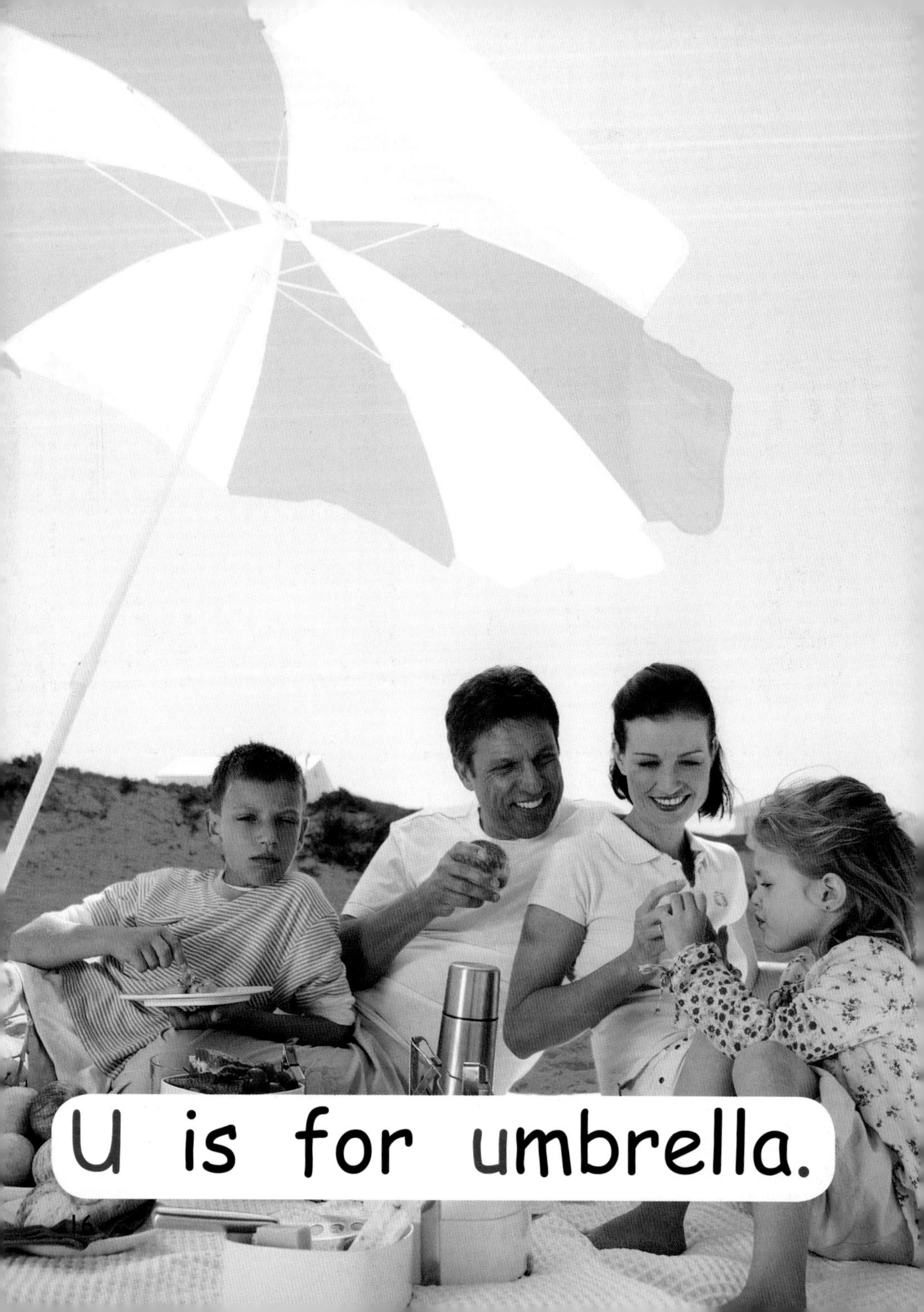

U is for umbrella.